Two Talks on Writing

John Crowley

Two Talks on Writing copyright © 2024
by John Crowley. All rights reserved.

Ninepin Press
75 Clark Street
Easthampton, MA 01027
ninepinpress.com
info@ninepinpress.com

ISBN 979-8-9897603-1-2 (paperback)
ISBN 979-8-9897603-2-9 (ebook)

"Practicing the Arts of Peace" first appeared in *Conjunctions* 46.

Printed in the United States on 100% recycled paper. Cover art: *Trompe-l'œil à la gravure de Sarrabat* (detail) by Jean Valette-Penot.

This book is one of four volumes comprising John Crowley's Conway Miscellany.

Contents

Practicing the Arts of Peace   5

The Uses of Allegory   38

Practicing the
Arts of Peace

The idea of a category that could be named "the arts of peace" and practiced under that rubric arose for me sometime in 2005, when I received an invitation from my old university to deliver an address, or lecture, about a topic of my choice, which was a surprise to me and an honor: I hadn't returned to Indiana for many years. What could I now say to the collected faculty and others come to hear this yearly address, named for the beloved Indiana governor and Democrat elder Roger Branigin?

About then I got an e-mail from an MFA candidate in writing at the University of Massachusetts, near where I live. I knew Andre slightly from parties and as a clerk in the best bookstore in Amherst. I can place the time of the letter by his first reference: *I've been bummed since Susan Sontag died*, he wrote (that had happened at the end of the year before). *For me, she is the most important intellectual. . . . It's weird trying to mourn for someone who you didn't know but who changed you so much (and the world, for that matter). So—I don't know, how do you mourn Susan Sontag? Read a novel by someone from Eastern Europe? Watch a German film? Go to the ballet? Go to Iraq? It seems so stupid to even try . . .*

He continued then: *I wonder—if you don't mind me asking such a dreadful question—where you think your work fits in the world. And I don't mean "the world of letters"—I mean the world. . . . What do you think it's doing out there, set adrift? What do you hope it's doing? Maybe you don't hope it's doing anything, really—but I would guess that you do.*

I didn't answer for some time, and when I did it was without much thought—or maybe with the distillation of a lot of thought that had been going on below the level of even mental speech. "Andre," I wrote at last, "I was asked by somebody back at the time of the invasion of Iraq how we could all just go on writing our little stories, especially we fantasists and poets, and I said that in my opinion what we were doing is practicing the arts of peace. What we want is a world in which fantastical stories are possible and are valued, in which there is nothing so dreadful or urgent that it causes the writing of such things to stop or to be stopped. Worlds where the arts of peace can't be practiced are wounded worlds, and that's why we have to go on practicing those arts, so that our worlds don't die. Bruno Schulz in the Poland of World War II practiced the arts of peace in his fantastic stories—until he was killed. No one's likely to kill me for being a practitioner, but it's what I do." This reply now seems to me so compressed as to be not entirely intelligible, and yet it is the answer I meant to give: the answer it consisted of then, and what it means in the thought-world I live in now.

First of all, what had I meant then by

"the arts of peace"? I didn't mean artworks that plead for or promote peace, or denounce injustice or hatred or violence. I meant something like the opposite of that, or at least at ninety degrees from it. I was thinking of works that have no designs upon us, that do not aim to convince or convert or instruct us; works that follow their own aesthetic imperatives and no others, works that are good but can't really be said to do good, that are superfluous to the economics and politics of utility, though they may be commodities, even popular ones in high demand. The arts of peace flourish in times of peace, and their flourishing marks an age of peace—or at least a space, or a hope, or an assumption of peace, or maybe only a nostalgia for such a space or time: they assert the possibility of a space of peace by their existence. That's their only utility, though not their value.

Of all the arts of peace, music has the least need to justify the production of works that have only their own aesthetic demands to meet, which is why Walter Pater said that all art aspires to the condition of music. Bach's cantatas and masses are intended to promote or intensify religious feeling, but—unlike religious tracts or religious novels—they have very similar effects on those who are not religious, and his secular or nonutilitarian music has no reference except itself. Operas, from Verdi to John Adams and Philip Glass, may have designs on us, and be concerned with liberty, injustice, tyranny, and violence, but they all need words and narrative to make their points, as do songs—the indifference of music to import can be shown by the way the same melody can support words of widely varied meaning. Rossini used the same overture for different operas, serious and comic.

Narrative arts though—stories, dramas, films—are never free of connections to our lived lives, the human predicament, the age or the social moment; they have to tell stories *about* something, and it's been shown now by a century of experiment that they die if they don't. Most people would agree that bringing us news, or instruction, or descriptions of our own or other social structures, or explication of our dilemmas and moral challenges, is a big part of what stories do and should do. Those that are effective at this work need to have no other power, and some of them have had great power: they really do make things happen. Fictions that have had such power in the world tend to lose it when the world changes, and they cease to be read much, like Upton Sinclair's *The Jungle*, which altered the meat-packing industry and made Spam safe both to make and to eat. Nikolay Chernyshevsky's 1863 political novel *What Is to Be Done?* (wonderfully spoofed by Vladimir Nabokov in *The Gift*) inspired a generation of Russian reformers, but couldn't now. *1984* is an exception, maybe, somehow still horribly powerful as parable though its particular lessons are outdated. But *Les Miserables* doesn't send us to the barricades now, any more than *Gone with the Wind* makes us supporters of white supremacy, as it surely was meant to do. If they are still read, they are read for a different reason and hold the attention in a different way. They die as social power and flow into the sea of stories; they join the great majority—those many many works that merely build worlds of words, set imaginary people off on adventures, resolve pretend dilemmas in unlikely ways that we find strangely gratifying, and always have: we need them, though we can't perhaps say why, or what good they are; and the making of them, the making of them well on their own terms and according to their own imperatives, is one of the arts of peace. It's the one I try to practice.

My earliest master was Vladimir Nabokov; that is to say, I had always been a consumer of tales in many forms, was from an early age enamored by the *Alice* books, Sherlock Holmes, EC comics, and John

Wayne films, and also biographies of assorted people and nature stories; I was always someone who, as Andre Gide said of himself, tended to be more moved by the representations of things than by things themselves. I discovered or maybe rather uncovered Nabokov when I was fifteen and read *Lolita* in secret, thinking it was a dirty book, which of course it is and certainly was for a boy not much older than Lolita; but what took me more was the language artifact that it was, the thing of words, the scheme of puns and jokes and cross-references and delicate put-downs and anagrams, many of which I could sense but not get, yet somehow would rise into an agonizing delight. I knew that the book wasn't only about a perverse love affair but entirely about itself; the shocking subject was really just a way of raising the bar of difficulty.

Nabokov is a great writer, and his books are an education, but he may be a bad mentor. With him I learned to hold in contempt teachers who asked, "What is the author's purpose?" or worse, "What is this guy trying to say?" and to despise symbols and allegories and "Freudian voodooism." With him I rejected the Literature of Ideas and (having read little or nothing of them) rejoiced in dismissing Balzac, Gorki, and Thomas Mann, as well as the "hopelessly banal and enormous novels typed out by the thumbs of tense mediocrities and called 'powerful' and 'stark' by reviewing hacks" that he also mocks. (I did later come to admire Faulkner, whom Nabokov labeled a "corncob humorist.") "For me," he writes, "a novel exists only insofar as it affords me what I shall bluntly call *aesthetic bliss*, that is, a sense of being somehow, somewhere, connected with other states of being where art (curiosity, tenderness, kindness, ecstasy) is the norm. *Don Quixote* is a fairy tale, so is *Bleak House*, so is *Dead Souls*. *Madame Bovary* and *Anna Karenina* are supreme fairy tales. But without these fairy tales the world would not be real."

. . .

I'm not certain of the chronology, but it's possible that Nabokov's champagne cocktail of word and Eros drew me out of the imagined worlds I then lived in: the puppet theater, the lesser Elizabethans, the narrative poems of Swinburne, the romantic tragedies whose contents I imagined more than I actually read. If that's so, then the germ lay dormant a long time; in college I sent away my other-worldly urges and read Camus and Sartre and other Literature of Ideas, studied photography and planned to make movies. Not until I was in my mid-twenties did I begin on an enterprise of a different kind, and far removed (as I thought) from any kind of literature. It was about the distant future, a kind of melancholy autumnal Eden, where there were no arts of peace or any arts at all because there was peace itself instead, perpetual peace. There were stories, though; in fact stories were this society's history, religion, amusement, and truth; the highest ambition, in a world almost without ambition, was to be a teller of true stories, indeed finally to become the stories you tell. Which is what happens to the teller of my story. That book (when it eventually appeared as a book, much chastened, years later) was called *Engine Summer*. It had less to do with Nabokov's austere aestheticism than with the era's Edenic longings and willed detachment from history.

Even before it was entirely finished, I had begun thinking of another book, a fairy tale that was actually a long novel in the realist tradition, a "family chronicle" like *Buddenbrooks* or *The Wapshot Chronicle*. Unlike the usual family chronicle, mine would begin in the present and go on into the future, as the world evolved in strange ways I would devise. I say it was conceived as a fairy tale, but in fact the idea that it would contain actual fairies themselves came rather late in my thinking—a way of raising the bar, to see if I could make readers take the little fairies of Victorian and Elizabethan imaginings seriously; to make an imaginary garden with real fairies at the bottom of it. The eventual book was called *Little, Big: or, The Fairies' Parliament*, which I thought was expressive of its nature, but the publisher who first issued it had concerns: this was to be a book for general readers, not merely readers of fantasy. It didn't do very well in its initial appearance as a general fiction title, but when it was reissued as clearly a fairy-tale of some kind, it migrated to the back of the bookstore, where the kinds of books are kept for readers who read no other kind. It has lately returned to the general-reader shelves for people to find who rarely or never read that kind.

What kind?

It was back when I was in the midst of writing it that I myself discovered what kind of book or story mine was, and why it worked as it did, and to what course or stream of the human imaginative enterprise it belonged to and had poured from, and that was when I read the great Canadian critic Northrop Frye's book *The Secular Scripture: A Study of the Structure of Romance.*

Frye asserted that as far back as there has been narrative, there have been two strands: those stories we deem to be true, among which are sacred scriptures and tales that can also be described as myths: tales that tell us how the world came to be, why we die and what comes after, why there are men and women, and so on; and another strand, a *secular* scripture equally important to us and perhaps primitively not different from the sacred, but whose truth is not important—stories told for their own sakes, to amuse, amaze, and thrill. There is a naive and a sentimental variety of these, in Schiller's terms. The naive is the mass of fable and folktale passed at first orally. Those tales intertwine with the sentimental, that is, stories consciously composed and written down, whose origins Frye traces to the late Greeks. All these tales collectively Frye calls *romances*, a family of stories that (like any family) can't be defined but only characterized, and whose characteristic story shapes and structures, devices, and outcomes are so many that works within the family can share none at all, and yet we sense that they belong together. Heroes with hidden parentage, journeys to win treasure or redeem honor, often leading into dark underworlds of entrapment and repetition, labyrinths and prisons; lovers separated and united, girl meets boy, boy loses girl, girl gets boy; twins, doubles, mistaken identities resolved; weddings that turn winter into spring, talking animals, riddles and prophecies; supernatural agencies good and bad. Stories not all with happy endings yet in which somehow the algebra of imagining comes out right, balancing the dark world we fear and don't want with the good world we do want—the world (as Frye puts it) that our gods would want for us if they were worth worshiping.

What I had written was a romance; those books in the back of the store and on the special-tastes shelves were romances, for sale to those who knew just what they were looking for; but so were many of those in the front of the store, bought by readers who knew what they wanted when they got it but maybe not before. They are the kinds of stories that Plato would have none of in his Republic. Plato's strictures descend into Western Christendom, which is faced with what to do about the vast mass of story, folklore, and fable that interpenetrates its own teachings. The Renaissance rediscovering the great body of ancient romance also reestablished Plato's neat idea that these thrilling wonder stories about the doings of gods and heroes and lovers could be understood *allegorically*, containing hidden morals that can be teased out (*what is this guy trying to say?*) and so be made acceptable to serious people. The head would—as it should—take charge of the heart and show how the tales that the heart loves can also improve us: at least some of them can. When the Western narrative tradition divided again, into romantic and realistic (never completely and in some ways not at all), the same division into imaginary stories that are instructive and those that are not persists: trash is trash, but some good stories are also good for you. Recent serious readers in this tradition have preferred mystery stories to other kinds of romances, especially the *noir* kind, as containing more information about real life than others; but many extravagant fantasies are *noir* as well.

Our culture is stuffed with fantasy and romances in potent new media not invented when Plato fretted over the question of the utility of stories—or when I began planning such stories. Cultural critics, unused to making discriminations among the works they encounter into better and lesser according to a Nabokovian aesthetic, tend to rank them instead by their truth-telling qualities. Those most disconnected from our shared social universe and its physics and politics, and most frank in the deployment of tropes of romance, were classed as *escapist*: a word that implies that those who spend too much time within them are evading or forswearing the duty we all have to work for justice or betterment or at least survival.

There is a case to be made, too: the old Irish Celts, who have been conceived of as dreamy and romantic, perceived a danger in the attraction to other worlds, worlds of delight, excitement, and gratified desire, and represented the danger in the many tales about what becomes of careless wanderers who allow themselves to be drawn into the land of the fairies within the earth: they emerge years later, pale and empty-eyed, no older or more mature than when they went in and having gained nothing except a permanent dissatisfaction with the everyday world that their coevals have been all along struggling with—sort of like young people emerging from years of obsession with *Star Wars* or video games or, well, *fairies*, reading tome upon huge tome of news from Neverland and never growing any older.

As I tried, back in the century's first years, to explain what it meant to practice the arts of peace, I thought such practice may not only be said to be no help to the world, it may be open to condemnation as inducements to abandon it. To picture worlds that are either Edenic and impossible, or lawless and in ruins, might be to weaken a reader's allegiance to the world as it is and the possibilities it really contains, particularly for those whose connection to it is tenuous to begin with.

A more serious charge can be made against worlds made of words and stories, worlds that have innocence at their hearts or centers because they are incapable of harm. Works that have not done good can be implicated in the doing of evil. In the high/low critique, those works that don't teach us about real life, directly or allegorically, are simply useless, ignorable; modern Platonists, though, using the tools of deconstruction and the New Historicism, discover that works which seem to connect us to realms where curiosity, tenderness, and ecstasy are the norm are at their core simply coded illustrations of their society's actual power relationships—"who whom," in Lenin's formulation: who has done harm to, or stolen from, whom; who has despised whom, or defined whom as lesser for reasons of gain, or obliterated from sight in order to retain power. It can all be discovered, in the romances, ghost stories, melodramas, and revels that seem like merely ephemeral fun. This clear-sighted watchfulness is opposite to the response of the helpless escapist, now seen as not only ineffectual but complicit in wrongs that are merely masked by the works he tries to escape into.

Well, how can the making of romances as an art of peace refute this charge, supposing we want to refute it, without saying well we don't care, we like it, and it makes us feel good to create and "consume" it and the knowers-better can go elsewhere, or rather *we* can, we can escape into the hills of Gondor and the pathetic fallacies of fantasy; but that's only to become the charge we want to meet. "Better is the sight of the eye than the wanderings of desire," says Ecclesiastes. Hamlet says that the business of art, of theater art anyway, is to hold the mirror up to nature, to "show Virtue her own feature, scorn her own image, and the very age and body of the time his form and pressure." But of course the most important thing about the image in any mirror is that it's reversed, as Lewis Carroll knew, and opposite to what it reflects. Perhaps this can point us to an escape, from escapism as well as from Knowing Better: Couldn't it be that those works (like Shakespeare's comedies, the pastorals of Watteau, the fantasies of Ronald Firbank and Giacomo Puccini) are not evasive encodings of social power, inauthentic assertions of freedom canceled out by the very contradictions they are created to hide, but are actually conscious mirror-reversals of those dilemmas that we suffer—social, cultural, political, maybe biological or mammalian even? That could be instructive in itself, a revelation, like that famous map you can buy that shows the Western Hemisphere upside down, with Tierra del Fuego and the South Pole at the top and our own weirdly diminished country looking rather insignificant toward the bottom. Creating a world where power has no power, where only love has power—does it refresh our senses somehow, so we can see more clearly our life on earth, where (as we all know very well) power indeed has power, and love is often, maybe usually, not enough?

Well, I don't know. I think this reversal effect really does describe some of the pull that romances and allied arts have on us, like the hilarious reversals of a joke, or the train wrecks and car crashes impossibly escaped or avoided in a Buster Keaton film that would never be escaped in life. Whether experiencing such gratifying reversals of our actual condition really does us good, or makes us better, is not indicated by what I know of world history. We have all heard of the death-camp commandant moved to tears by Mozart and Beethoven in his spare time; Saddam Hussein was the author of a couple of tender romances about love and honor.

So I don't really want to state that the arts of peace can oppose strong evil and by their cunning innocence neutralize that caustic energy. The arts of peace can't save the world; it's more the case that the world must save them. They are like the proverbial miner's canary: when we see it dead, when the arts of peace have declined, or been corrupted, or are despised or co-opted, as they can so easily be, then we should think about backing out and heading for the upper air.

And yet I still can't help believing that

to *practice* the arts of peace, these small and seemingly futile arts without effect, is to create, or help to keep in existence, or at the very least to assert the possibility of the world we want: a world in which not all our time is spent in vigilance, or in fending off danger, or in struggle with corruption or stupidity, or in the education of the heart by the head so that we can do those tasks.

In fact I'll assert more than that: I think that in the darkest of worlds which have arisen in this and in other centuries, to practice the arts of peace as I have tried to describe them may well be heroic, and salvific too. The Cuban poet and journalist Raúl Rivero became a dissident and critic of the Castro regime after working for a long time as a dutiful foreign correspondent. After 1991 he began to campaign for reforms like those that had altered Eastern Europe and Russia, and was a signatory of the famed "Carta de los Dies," and began sending out accounts of life in Cuba to foreign presses. He was growing well-known throughout the Latin American world, but he was jobless, without resources, living on the odd check that would make its way to him. Whenever a foreign journalist came to interview or visit him and asked, "What can I do for you?" Rivero would answer, "Leave me your pen."

Arrested at last, Rivero was sentenced to twenty years in prison. He was afraid, he said, and even more he was afraid of his own fear. "I was afraid of not being able to stand it," he wrote later. "Everything is programmed to undo you as a human being." Even his jailers understood his stature as poet and critic, and with an almost Kafkaesque ingenuity, they permitted him to go on writing—with the condition that he could write only love poems.

He didn't find it easy, at first. But he began to write, and as he did so, he began, he says, to remember the many, many women he had loved, married, hadn't married, lost, or left; and every time he finished one, he felt that his captors had not defeated him.

His jailers read through the poems each week, confiscating those that they thought had a secret message or were somehow inflammatory—though Rivero said he had no idea what in any poem might excite their suspicion. He only wrote on.

International pressure on the Cuban government finally freed Rivero, who lives now in Spain. His prison love poems have been published to some acclaim—a rarity, he says, a book of love poems edited by the police. The name of the volume is *Corazón sin Furia*—a heart without rage.

By himself and in the face of his fears he projected, in that cold cell, a world where power has no power: where love has power. With luck and some genius it may outlast the world of his jailers.

Another prison story: Grigory Pasko, a military reporter and captain in the Russian Navy's Pacific Fleet, observed Russian Navy tankers dumping nuclear wastes in the sea off Vladivostok near the Japanese islands. Pasko filmed the violations and wrote about them, passing his film to Japanese television. The Russian government arrested and tried Pasko in secret and sent him to prison. After nearly two years, during which Pasko continued to assert his innocence, the Russian government became embarrassed enough to grant him amnesty, reducing his charge to misuse of office and letting him go. Pasko, however, rejected the offered pardon. "No one could convince me I broke the law," he said.

The Russian government brought new charges against the uncooperative Pasko, and after another secret treason trial (he was supposed to have been a Japanese spy), Pasko was given a four-year sentence at Prison Colony No. 41, a labor prison near the town of Ussuriisk. "Gray, black, and dirty brown," he remembers the place being: that colorless place that I can guess few or none of us here have ever been condemned to but which we all know, which we all have dreamed of, the gray places of the gray Gulag that snakes across our human history. Amnesty International took up Pasko's case, calling it "a clear breach of national and international norms protecting freedom of expression that the Russian state is obliged to uphold." Amnesty International members began sending Pasko letters of support, and picture postcards, from around the world—some 24,000 in all. He says he has saved them all. The letters were encouraging but the pictures on the postcards were just as helpful: "Many of them were beautiful and bright," he remembers. "The sky, the sea, water, green grass. All the prisoners would come over and look at these postcards from Amnesty International." He put many of them up on his gray wall, a shifting gallery, maybe the Rockies or the Alps at sunset, the Eiffel Tower lit up, castles and countrysides and beaches, the fabulous unreal worlds within postcards that make all of us smile and long without pain—sometimes even those of us who live amid those very scenes. Pasko was released from prison in January 2003, but it was for good behavior and not a reversal of his conviction.

A third story: There was in Japan once — it is said — a famous master of the tea ceremony or *chado*, which ranks among the arts of peace if anything does. One day, an unscrupulous *ronin* or outlaw samurai challenged the *chado* master to a duel — knowing full well that the *chado* master had no skill in martial arts, perhaps hoping for a bribe, or merely indulging a love of bullying. The *chado* master accepted the challenge and agreed to meet the *ronin* the next day. He then went to the house of a well-known samurai to ask for help. I know, he told the warrior, that I will be quickly killed by this fellow, but I would like to be able at least to die with dignity and not look a fool before the world. Could the samurai give him some basic instructions, a stance to take, a lesson in holding a weapon properly? The samurai said that perhaps he could do so, if the *chado* master wished; and then he requested that, since the man was to die tomorrow, he make tea for him, perhaps for the last time in his life. That evening then, the *chado* master made tea for the samurai with all the composure and perfection of his decades of practice. The samurai, having observed the *chado* master's absorption and calm, told him that the only advice he had for him was this: that he should engage in his battle with the ronin as though the man were a guest for whom he was making tea. He gave the *chado* master a sword he could use, and said that he thought all would be well. The next day at the appointed time the ronin appeared, ready to fight. The *chado* master said that he was ready too. He began his preparations for the battle just as he would his preparations for tea. He made his bow; he took off his outer garment and folded it with care in the prescribed manner, without hurry or fuss. He laid his fan upon it with the practiced gesture. The ronin, observing his complete self-possession, began to be afraid: What did this fellow know that made him so cool? The *chado* master reached to take up the borrowed sword with the same calmness of mind and full attention as he would have the implements of his art, and at that the ronin began to lose his nerve — surely no one about to die could be so unafraid — perhaps he was a secret martial arts master as well — and suddenly convinced he could never defeat the man, the ronin fled.

This story is, obviously, different from the other two. The prison stories are true, though the telling of them may bring forth a point or a vision that they didn't have when they were *simply* true, that is, before they were stories. The story of the *chado* master who defeated brutal power with the arts of peace may be nothing *but* a story: not a distilled incident from the world's life but merely a hopeful parable — one of those which assert such an impossible, Utopian success for the arts of peace that on hearing it all we can do is smile. But that's all it needs to do. It is in itself an example of the thing it teaches.

• • •

Northrop Frye, in his study of Shakespearean comedy, defines the effects of different modes of narrative in a way that I think is crucial. In watching tragedy, he says—and within tragedy I would include all that is serious, critical, alerting in fiction from *Middlemarch* to *1984* and the stories of Alice Munro—we are impressed by the *reality of the illusion*: we feel that the blinding of Gloucester in *King Lear* is not really happening, but it is the kind of thing that can and does happen, and this is what it would be like to witness it. Our response to comedy is different—and within comedy I would include all tales of Eden restored, of the lineaments of gratified desire, glittering gay serpents with their tails in their mouths, happy though not all with happy endings. In comedy, Frye says, we are impressed with the *illusion of reality*: this is the sort of thing that just doesn't happen—and yet here it is, happening. I will believe such experiences are not escapist, that seeing before us the world we *want* can give us heart to bring the world we *have* closer to it, or keep it from impossibility at least—I believe it, but I won't assert it. I will assert this: the arts of peace may make nothing happen, but a world that cannot afford the arts of peace, or despises them as trivial or inauthentic, that corrupts them or makes their practice impossible, is not a world of unfooled hardworking realists but a counter-world: a world in which the real ambiguity, the real multiplicity, the unfinishable endlessness of real things can't be truly seen.

So that is what I hope the effect of my work has been, and I will take responsibility for it, though I anticipate its actual effect to be general indifference. I would like to open to my readers a realm where curiosity, tenderness, and ecstasy are the norm, or at the very least a realm where they seem possible: the lost child saved, the lovers who find each other at last; the world evolving, out of the past we know, a present different from the one we have; the triumph of love over power; and say to my readers, "Look! This can't happen—but here it is, happening."

The Uses of Allegory

I have been thinking about allegory recently, in no particularly rigorous way, since being invited to speak to Mythcon attendees in 2019; in the end I was unable to attend the con and read my remarks over the Internet. (COVID had not yet brought Zoom into worldwide attention. This piece is a modified version of what I read.)

Some definitions are in order. Allegory in some ways resembles symbolism, and symbolism reflects metaphor but isn't the same. Symbols can have actuality, can even have recorded histories, and can appear in varied ways in fictions. Lots of symbols live with us in our world: flags, monuments, uniforms, advertising icons. Cemetery sculptures have symbolic power, representations of resurrection, mourning, consolation. *Literary* symbols refer to matters within the story they furnish. In Michael Arlen's 1920s novel *The Green Hat*, the hat is a symbol for racy young people throwing off the previous generation's rules and prejudices. Metaphors can illuminate moments in stories, but refer to nothing but that illumination. *Allegories*, however, are fictional stories that exist only in that they are attached to other realities, other stories: moral commandments, the practice of justice and mercy, truths that stand at a remove from and "higher" than the allegorical story that points to them. Often what is pointed to in an allegory is another story, a more urgent or important story, usually one the reader knows in another context. A story out of the New Testament can be allegorized in a story set in the present day, or on another planet, while being itself an allegory of divine love or charity.

Allegory is likely the least loved of all literary forms, and even when the two tracks of the allegory are gripping in some way, the obviousness of the enterprise is always a little annoying. The writer attempting allegory needs to create an interesting and challenging story on the base level, while constantly allowing in pointers to the true matter, which in almost all allegories isn't fictional but moral, or political, or religious. C. S. Lewis wrote a great and lasting book about the possibilities of allegory throughout Western literature, and he wrote some himself; in fact it might be said that all his fiction was allegorical in some sense.

A key moment in the reading of an allegory (whether the reader perceives the story as an allegory or does not) is the reader's growing awareness of what is allegorized. When I was in high school, sixty years ago, I read a couple of Lewis's planetary romances: *Out of the Silent Planet*, *Perelandra*. Lewis was then admired and even cherished by Catholics, lay and clerical, and though my family was Catholic, *I* read the novels because they were science fiction, though it turned out they actually weren't. When I realized that they were actually *allegories*—though I didn't know much then about the category, or could have explained it—I was deeply annoyed. What value was there in undercutting the aesthetics of SF, which in both books were striking and compelling, to produce what any Christian could easily decode? I knew the story of Adam and Eve; I understood the battle of the angels; I needed no lessons in the matter of original sin. Much later on I read *The Allegory of Love* and then understood the attraction the SF project held for Lewis: the novels were what Lewis labelled "the marvellous-known-to-be-fiction." As he explains: "For poetry to spread its wings fully, there must be, besides the believed religion, a marvellous that knows itself as myth. For this to come about, the old marvellous . . . must be stored up somewhere. Such a sleeping-place was provided for the gods by allegory . . . for gods, like other creatures, must die to live."

The pagan gods, and the stories told about them, are mostly allegories of nature: astral objects, the oceans, vegetation, strife, death, sex—"whatever is begotten, born, and dies," as Yeats says. In the Western world, the allegorical gods come in time to be replaced (or at least sidelined) by growing monastic theology: by abstractions, named concepts like Mens, Natura, Pietas, Amor, etc. But those named concepts, when painted by Giotto, or called on to speak in medieval writings, take on the allegorical functions that the gods were forced to relinquish when they went to sleep. The visual representations of those theological abstractions, with their symbols, form in effect the allegory of an allegory.

The Christian belief is that nature is "fallen" and that our natures are not only implicated in the fall of nature but brought about by our own fall into disobedience. The events of that story—snake, apple, fig leaf—can be understood as an allegory of a spiritual fall. Once in an ethics class in college, taught by a Jewish refugee professor and biblical scholar, I disputed the value or force of that story; I did not believe we humans had been exiled from or deprived of a unified realm where all the other animals remained. But we *had*, he said; we came down out of the trees (!) and over time lost our original innocence, or ignorance; we came to know that we would die—all animals die, but other animals almost certainly don't envision it; we do, and the knowledge has been a vast force in human life on earth. We can't return to a place or time where we don't know we will die, or don't know we are naked. It might be said that the Biblical story allegorizes the division of human consciousness from animal consciousness in the growing understanding that we are not in nature. An original perfection or "innocence" of which we were once a part was corrupted, both in the sense of putting nature to our own uses, and in our knowledge that we are born to die.

These two qualities of allegory—the story told and the matter it indicates—makes allegory both powerful and weak when deployed in fiction. What Lewis terms "the marvelous known to be fiction"—what the great Canadian critic Northrop Frye called "the secular scripture"—has gained immense power lately, partly due to advancing technologies of entertainment, but possibly also for more moral reasons. A lot of fantasy films deploying CGI and animation to create obvious versions of dozens of ancient stories can be called allegories—but allegories of what? Adam and Eve certainly turn up with some frequency in the new storytelling, as do battles of good angels and evil angels, God and Satan, dark and light, Heaven and Hell, in a thousand forms, some using those old signifiers directly, some not, but insofar as they are versions of the Christian or Biblical stories, the new stories can also be seen as allegories of an allegory. I've often thought that while realist fictions are full of struggles between persons whose moral and spiritual parts are mostly hidden or unfixed, liable to change as plots evolve, *fantasy* fiction gets to embody the same moral or spiritual energies in things—not only in weapons, a big category, but in magic helpers, recovered ancestral gifts, journeys of courage, all of it shown on the surface: in symbolic things, the inside is made outside, and outside actions and powers allegorize the inside. Allegory in this sense is easy to use but hard to make new: superheroes who work to save lesser souls from the snares of evil beings can also sin, lose their powers, becoming ordinary mortals (for a time). They are instantly interpretable: we get it.

Belief systems of many kinds present their tenets and their stories as actually existing or occurring in the world: in the beginning of everything; in the time of the reception of the faith and its new description of reality; and also now. These assumed existent things—divine or supernatural beings and their activities and operations—can be allegorized secondarily in stories that restate, in more obvious or accessible forms, the mystic truths and beings that abide in a primary realm of their own. Over time, such a belief system can lose its grip on the imagination *as a set of actualities* and in effect become immured in "the sleeping-place of the gods" that Lewis defined. Linguistic or artistic allegories that were at first adopted solely as pointers or coded aspects of divinity or morality can, in the end, comprise all there is of the system. What is interesting to me is that when a realm of divine beings, laws, activities, and judgments passes away, their *allegorical* power, which now points to nothing but itself, doesn't necessarily lose its *spiritual* power.

Take Gnosticism, which comes in many flavors and offers more than one example of this process. Central to many gnostic systems is the belief that we humans are divine beings who once inhabited a realm of light outside the physical cosmos. We suffered a fall or an eviction from that realm (different gnostic sects give different reasons for this fall) and were cast into the dark and cold realm of the physical, and the physical body. Mandaean gnosticism posits numerous dark worlds into which the soul can sink, getting ever farther from "the house of my parents" and "lost among the worlds." I was very moved by the Mandaean system and its more sophisticated forms when I learned about it. I turned what I got from it and similar gnostic teachings not only into the underlying affective structure of a book but the source for a comic strip that a character in the book follows: *Little Enosh: Lost Among the Worlds*. The Mandaean cast of characters became characters in the strip: Enosh (sometimes Anosh or Enoch in the original texts) is a spaceman, appearing to be a young boy who wanders in worlds where he is never at home. On these planets Enosh is caught and imprisoned over and over (as he is in Gnostic imagining) by Rutha, an evil queen, sometimes Ruha in the texts, and her bad-guy gang, the Uthras, who aren't exactly bad guys in the original myth. Rutha wants above all for imprisoned Enosh to admit she is his mother, but he won't because she isn't. Enosh is rescued from the Inn of the Worlds (an actual Mandaean term for the dark and confining universe we live in, or have been "thrown into," as the texts have it) by his actual mother, Amanda D'Haye, whom I derived from the Mandaean gnostic figure Manda d'Hayye, personified knowledge from the Worlds of Light. (I pictured her as resembling Olive Oyl. Enosh in his spaceship is reminiscent of *Calvin and Hobbes*'s Spaceman Spliff.) I've never had more fun in writing than I did in learning how the Mandean texts could form an allegorical background for ordinary modern people and doings.

Not all allegory is religious, but it does seem to require a certain seriousness, at least for its original readers (or viewers;

pictorial art can be allegorical in some ways more easily than story can; see William Blake). Nor does allegory have to be extensive. An example would be the Owl of Minerva. Hegel, whose conception it is, says that the Owl of Minerva takes wing only at dusk. What he intends to express (almost all allegories need explication) is that only in its decline can we understand the true nature of a society or an age or an epoch. "Minerva's owl" comprises Minerva's attributes of wisdom, logos, reason, memory. It's flight in the gray dusk is used not only to stand for the decline, and conceive the fall, of an age, but also to perceive the qualities of the epoch or age to come. Minerva's owl flies at a time when an old age is dying and a new age is struggling to be born. Minerva's owl could be called a metaphor, but it seems to express too large an idea to be simply that. It's an allegory: it wakes, it perceives the dusk, it flies, it knows the night and is certain of the dawn. I recently read a long and fascinating piece in the *New York Times*. It tells of an unmarried, "spiritual but not religious" professional in her early 30s who moved out of her communal house and into a convent of the Sisters of Mercy. A bunch of friends went with her. They called their project Nuns and Nones, and they were the "Nones"—progressive millennials, none practicing Catholics, most interested in some form of social justice work. Millennials are the least religious group in America—only 27 percent attend religious services weekly. These young people, mostly women and a few men, were seeking ways to live radical activist lives, lives of devotion to their causes. The sisters began to see that the millennials wanted a road map for life and ritual, rather than a belief system. On one of the first nights, Sister Judy Carle said, one of the young people casually asked the sisters not what they believed but "What's your spiritual practice?" Ritual, story, commitments to practice, spiritual friendship, meant more than dogma, even when some of the Nones turned seriously to Catholicism, even if not—in some sense—to belief.

Two things struck me about this story. First and most obvious was its resemblance to, or reproduction of, early monasticism: the Benedictine joining of prayer and work ("laborare est orare," to work is to pray) and the retreat of so many men and women from a collapsing world into safety and sense as much as into prayer and worship. And I had also begun to wonder if the "believed religion" (Lewis's term) of most of the West in the last 2,000 years is itself now becoming the "old marvellous that knows itself as myth" (as Lewis says of paganism) and will itself have to undergo the same resurrection: it may have to die to live. The central stories, practices, arts of what might be called "ceremonial Christianity" (as opposed to the bare Christianity of, say, Unitarianism or Quakerism) might survive the religion itself, while the belief-system and the cosmos that it expresses will revert to Lewis's "sleeping-place provided by allegory." Terry Eagleton, former Marxist literary critic, now Christian thinker, has said that "A sacrament is a sign that accomplishes what it signifies." I am thinking that an allegory—even the allegory that points to something no longer stable or powerful—might be regarded as a story which produces the realm that governs what it tells.